# 1985
# *The Year*
# *I Was Born*

Compiled by Sally Tagholm

Illustrated by Michael Evans

FANTAIL

in association with Signpost Books

FANTAIL
Published by the Penguin Group
Penguin Books Ltd, 27 Wrights Lane, London W8 5TZ, England
Penguin Books USA Inc., 375 Hudson Street, New York, NY 10014, USA
Penguin Books Australia Ltd., Ringwood, Victoria, Australia
Penguin Books Canada Ltd, 10 Alcorn Avenue, Toronto, Ontario, Canada
M4V 3B2
Penguin Books (NZ) Ltd, 182–190 Wairau Road, Auckland 10, New Zealand

Penguin Books Ltd., Registered Offices: Harmondsworth, Middlesex,
England

First published 1991
Published by Penguin Books in association with Signpost Books
10 9 8

Based on an original idea by Sally Wood
Conceived, designed and produced by Signpost Books Ltd, 1991
Copyright in this format © 1991 Signpost Books Ltd.,
25 Eden Drive, Headington, Oxford OX3 0AB, England

Illustrations copyright © 1991 Michael Evans
Text copyright © 1991 Sally Tagholm

Editor: Dorothy Wood
Art Director: Treld Bicknell
Paste up: Naomi Games

ISBN 1 874785 05 8 Hardback edition
ISBN 0140 90334 8 Paperback edition

Colour separations by Fotographics, Ltd.
Printed and bound in Belgium by Proost Book Production through
Landmark Production Consultants, Ltd.

Typeset by DP Photosetting, Aylesbury, Bucks

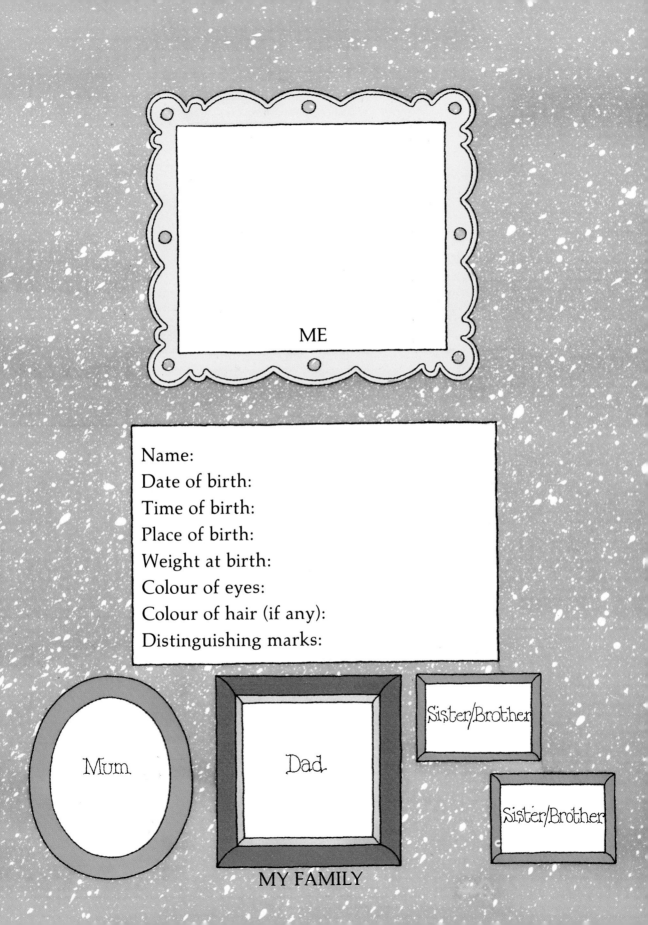

ME

Name:
Date of birth:
Time of birth:
Place of birth:
Weight at birth:
Colour of eyes:
Colour of hair (if any):
Distinguishing marks:

Mum

Dad

Sister/Brother

Sister/Brother

MY FAMILY

# January

| | |
|---|---|
| **Tuesday**<br>**January 1** | *The Times* newspaper's 200th birthday. The first edition (then called *The Daily Universal Register*) appeared on Jan 1 1785. |
| **Wednesday**<br>**January 2** | A new 50p coin is minted with the first new picture of the Queen for 17 years. It shows her in a diadem, necklace and drop earrings. |
| **Thursday**<br>**January 3** | Mrs Thatcher and Arthur Scargill are voted 'People of the Year' by BBC Radio 4's 'Today' programme. |
| **Friday**<br>**January 4** | British and Australian scientists using the infra-red telescope at Mauna Kea, Hawaii, say that they've found a Black Hole at the centre of the Milky Way. |

Snow and black ice in London and the Home Counties.

| | |
|---|---|
| **Saturday**<br>**January 5** | A plague of mites and beetles, including the Granary weevil and the Saw-toothed grain beetle, is threatening the bumper grain harvest from last year. |
| **Sunday**<br>**January 6** | It's so cold in Sussex that the rivers Ouse, Arun and Rother freeze. |
| **Monday**<br>**January 7** | Scientists from 30 countries attend International Conference on the future of Antarctica 724km from the South Pole on the Ross Ice Shelf.  Full Moon |
| **Tuesday**<br>**January 8** | So many people are slipping on the ice and breaking bones that they've run out of plaster of Paris at the Queen Alexandra Hospital in Cosham, Hants! The sea between Denmark and Sweden freezes. |
| **Wednesday**<br>**January 9** | A blackbird has laid an egg in the Christmas tree at Norwich Station. The station master won't take the tree down until the egg has hatched! |
| **Thursday**<br>**January 10** | Sir Clive Sinclair launches the C5—an electric tricycle with a top speed of 24kph. Four monkeys at Frankfurt Zoo in Germany are treated for frost-bitten tails. |
| **Friday**<br>**January 11** | The Greek government bans overweight people from driving. Driving licences will not be issued to anyone more than 70% heavier than normal. |
| **Saturday**<br>**January 12** | More than 10,000 ducks have been forced to land on the Orford marshes, Suffolk, because their Dutch wintering grounds are frozen. They are being fed with wheat. |

# January

Named after the Roman god Janus, who had two faces and could look backwards and forwards at the same time. Also known as 'frosty month', 'after-yule', 'first month' and 'snow month'.

## The Sinclair C5

The C5 is just over 1.8m long, is 73.6cm wide and 78.7cm high. It costs £399 and has a rechargeable battery which should last for about a year. It is classed as an electrically-assisted pedal cycle so can be driven by anyone over 14. You don't need a driving licence, number plate, seat belt or crash helmet and you don't have to pay road tax or insurance!

FLYING SCOTSMAN

GOLDEN ARROW

CHELTENHAM FLYER

**January 22:** PO issues stamps of five famous trains

ROYAL SCOT

CORNISH RIVIERA

### Cameras Roll!

Lord Orr-Ewing asks the first-ever publicly televised question in the House of Lords. He wants to know how many computers there are in schools now and how many teachers have been trained to teach children to use them. The Earl of Swinton gives the first-ever televised reply. He says that an estimated 80,000 microcomputers are in use in UK schools and that at least 120,000 teachers are trained to instruct in their use.

| | |
|---|---|
| *Sunday*<br>*January 13* | The Lord Mayor of London gives his annual Children's Fancy Dress Party at the Mansion House. |
| *Monday*<br>*January 14* | British Telecom launches a Halley's Comet Hotline. It gives information on the comet which will be intercepted in March 1986 by the European Space Agency's *Giotto* spacecraft. |
| *Tuesday*<br>*January 15* | The Big Freeze continues. The RSPCA organises the rescue of 50 dolphins and porpoises trapped in shallow water at Holmpton, North Humberside. |
| *Wednesday*<br>*January 16* | Opening of International Youth Year England at Coventry Cathedral. The Docklands Development Corporation announces a £1 billion scheme to build a new city 8km from the centre of London. |
| *Thursday*<br>*January 17* | British Telecom announces that they are going to abolish red telephone boxes, first introduced in 1927. |
| *Friday*<br>*January 18* | Blizzards in Dorset, Somerset, Devon and Cornwall; a Maximum Smog Alert in the Ruhr Valley in West Germany; and sandstorms in Egypt and Israel. |
| *Saturday*<br>*January 19* | RAF Hercules transport aircraft parachute men and equipment onto Salisbury Plain as part of Exercise Ice Axe. |
| *Sunday*<br>*January 20* | One of the 2 Blackfriars railway bridges across the river Thames, London, is demolished by a giant 800-tonne floating crane. |
| *Monday*<br>*January 21* | Thaw and flooding in southern England. The last animals move out as Southampton Zoo closes today. New Moon |
| *Tuesday*<br>*January 22* | The Post Office issues five new stamps of Famous Trains: the Flying Scotsman, the Golden Arrow, the Cheltenham Flyer, the Royal Scot and the Cornish Riviera. |
| *Wednesday*<br>*January 23* | The House of Lords is televised for the first time. US space shuttle *Discovery* is delayed by 24 hours because of ice on the launching tower at Cape Canaveral. |
| *Thursday*<br>*January 24* | Two men cross the English Channel in a hot-air balloon to celebrate the 200th anniversary of the first balloon crossing by Blanchard and Jefferies in 1785. It takes them 3hrs. |
| *Friday*<br>*January 25* | Neil Kinnock, the leader of the Labour party, eats pizza and baked beans for lunch at Oxstalls School, Gloucester. |

| | |
|---|---|
| **Saturday**<br>*January 26* | Australia Day. The Pope begins a 2-week tour of South America. |
| **Sunday**<br>*January 27* | US space shuttle *Discovery* lands perfectly at Kennedy Space Center in Florida, after a 3-day secret military mission. Britain's only sledge race round Loch an Eilean, near Aviemore in Scotland. |
| **Monday**<br>*January 28* | A record 4500 Bewick's Swans are spending the winter in the Ouse Washes, near Welney in Norfolk. They've flown over 3200km from Siberia. |
| **Tuesday**<br>*January 29* | Oxford University dons vote not to give an honorary doctorate to Mrs Thatcher. Britain announces that it will join a US project to launch a manned space station in 1992. |
| **Wednesday**<br>*January 30* | Scouts and Guides take part in a new nesting-box campaign in London to help birds whose natural habitats have been destroyed. |
| **Thursday**<br>*January 31* | Canada abandons compulsory metrication and gallons, pounds and inches become legal again! Vintage car rally starts from London to St Moritz to commemorate the centenary of the Cresta Run. |

**Blag**
THE SULTAN OF BRUNEI BUYS THE DORCHESTER HOTEL, LONDON, FOR £45,000,000

**Daily Owl**
NAVY BANS NYLON PANTS AT SEA

**Scandal**
NEW PROPOSALS TO PRESERVE STONEHENGE INCLUDE PLANS TO BUILD A FULL-SIZE REPLICA

**The Moon**
MOTH FOSSIL FROM DORSET COAST FOUND TO BE 180,000,000 YEARS OLD

# The Happy Birthday Page!

The Yeomen of the Guard are 400 years old
No 10 Downing Street is 250 years old
*The Times* newspaper is 200 years old
The Great Western Railway is 150 years old
The Salvation Army is 100 years old
The Mersey Tunnel is 100 years old
Cardiff Prison is 100 years old
The Cresta Run is 100 years old
The National Trust is 90 years old
The Girl Guide Association is 75 years old
The Volkswagen Beetle is 50 years old
Monopoly is 50 years old
The Ramblers' Association is 50 years old

# February

| | |
|---|---|
| *Friday*<br>*February 1* | Greenland is the first country to withdraw from the European Economic Community. It joined, with Denmark, in 1973. |
| *Saturday*<br>*February 2* | There are 3 earth tremors in Iran measuring 5.6 on the Richter Scale. |
| *Sunday*<br>*February 3* | 39th annual Clowns' Service at Holy Trinity Church, Dalston, East London. |
| *Monday*<br>*February 4* | The border between Gibraltar and Spain is reopened at midnight, after 16 years. A large school of porpoises is seen off the Isle of Wight. |
| *Tuesday*<br>*February 5* | The Chancellor of the Exchequer, Nigel Lawson, rules out the introduction of a plastic £1 note.     Full Moon |
| *Wednesday*<br>*February 6* | Richard Branson announces that he will challenge the Blue Riband speed record across the Atlantic in his 19.8m catamaran *Virgin Atlantic Challenger*.<br>35.6mm of rain at Cardiff (Rhoose) Airport. |
| *Thursday*<br>*February 7* | Temple Bar, which used to stand at the junction of the Strand and Fleet Street, London, but has been exiled to Hertfordshire for over 100 years, is to be re-erected in St Paul's Churchyard. |
| *Friday*<br>*February 8* | Snow in Wales, the Midlands and East Anglia. The 89th Crufts Dog Show opens at Earl's Court with a record entry of 11,141 dogs. |
| *Saturday*<br>*February 9* | A football match between Sheffield United and Oldham Athletic is postponed after a giant German bomb, one of 3 bombs that fell on Sheffield on December 12, 1940, is discovered.   Bomb |
| *Sunday*<br>*February 10* | Sub-zero temperatures. –5°C on Dartmoor. A standard poodle from Frensham, Surrey, called *Champion Montravia Tommy-Gun*, wins Best in Show title at Crufts. |
| *Monday*<br>*February 11* | The British Trust for Ornithology says that there are more rare Mandarin ducks in Britain than anywhere else in the world—at least 400 pairs. |
| *Tuesday*<br>*February 12* | The British Robot Association says that there are 2623 robots in Britain. The top 5 robot countries are Japan, USA, West Germany, France and Italy. |
| *Wednesday*<br>*February 13* | RSPCA cold weather warning: keep cats in; inspect dogs' paws for salt and grit and keep fish ponds clear of ice. |

| | |
|---|---|
| *Thursday*<br>*February 14* | St Valentine's Day. Concorde's first commercial flight from London to Sydney takes 17hrs 3mins 45secs. It's 7 hours faster than the previous record subsonic flight! |
| *Friday*<br>*February 15* | A new Guernsey flag flies in St Peter Port for the first time: it combines a gold cross, used by William the Conqueror, with the St George's Cross. |

# *February*

The Roman month of purification. The name comes from the Latin 'februo' which means 'I purify by sacrifice'. It has also been known as 'sprout kale' and 'rain month'.

## Chinese Year of the Buffalo

Chinese horoscopes follow a 12-year cycle, with each year represented by an animal. According to legend, the Buddha summoned all the animals to him one New Year, promising them a reward. Only 12 obeyed and he gave them each a year: the Rat arrived first, so he got the first year. The order is always the same—Rat, Buffalo, Tiger, Cat, Dragon, Snake, Horse, Goat, Monkey, Cockerel, Dog and Pig.

Buffaloes are quiet and patient. They are often very intelligent, and can make good leaders. They work hard and are good with their hands, but can be a bit stubborn! Buffaloes tend to be very traditional and are fond of their families. They get on well with Roosters and Rats but not with Monkeys, Goats or Tigers.

Famous Buffaloes include Aristotle, Richard the Lionheart, JS Bach, Louis XIII, Napoleon, Rubens, Van Gogh, Charlie Chaplin, Peter Sellers and Richard Burton.

### *How the Robot Got its Name*

In 1920, Czechoslovakian Karel Capek wrote a play called *R.U.R.* (Rossum's Universal Robots) about mechanical workers that developed their own intelligence, rebelled and exterminated the human beings. He called them robots from the Czech word for labour, *robota*.

| | |
|---|---|
| *Saturday*<br>*February 16* | United Nations famine relief operation sends 19 ships with 130,000 tonnes of food to Ethiopia. |
| *Sunday*<br>*February 17* | No smoking on London Underground stations that are partly or completely below ground. |
| *Monday*<br>*February 18* | 19 electronic parking meters with liquid crystal displays come into operation at Finsbury Circus in north London. |
| *Tuesday*<br>*February 19* | Pancake Day. Prince Andrew is 25; the National Trust is 90. Experts cause an artificial avalanche down the Eiger Wall in Switzerland to try to loosen massive build-up of snow.<br>New Moon |
| *Wednesday*<br>*February 20* | Beginning of Chinese Year of the Buffalo. Coastguards warn of mini-icebergs in the R Blackwater, Essex 4.5m long and 1.5m deep! |
| *Thursday*<br>*February 21* | About 16,000 competitors take part in a 200km skating marathon along the frozen canals of northern Holland. The winner finishes in 6hrs 47mins 44secs. |
| *Friday*<br>*February 22* | Neville Pickling, from Gainsborough, Lincs, catches a pike weighing 18.77kg on the Norfolk Broads, beating the British record of 18.16kg set 18 years ago. |
| *Saturday*<br>*February 23* | Blood oranges from Sicily, now called 'Ruby Reds', are back in the shops again after an absence of 15 years! |

9.8 hours of sunshine in Guernsey, Channel Isles.

| | |
|---|---|
| *Sunday*<br>*February 24* | Kettlewell Bridge, Wharfdale, collapses into the river Wharf. The B6160 between Grassington and Kettlewell is closed. |
| *Monday*<br>*February 25* | Experimental wheel clamping for illegal parking in central London is to carry on for another 2 years. |
| *Tuesday*<br>*February 26* | Two of the largest teachers' unions strike: 22,000 schools are affected. |
| *Wednesday*<br>*February 27* | The Prince of Wales opens NATO's £45m computerised naval control centre nearly 26m underground at Northwood, Middlesex. |
| *Thursday*<br>*February 28* | Robert Block (23), starts a sponsored run from Canterbury to Rome, Cairo and Jerusalem with letters of greeting from the archbishop to the Pope and other Church leaders. |

15.6°C at Valley, Anglesey.

# UK Fact File 1985

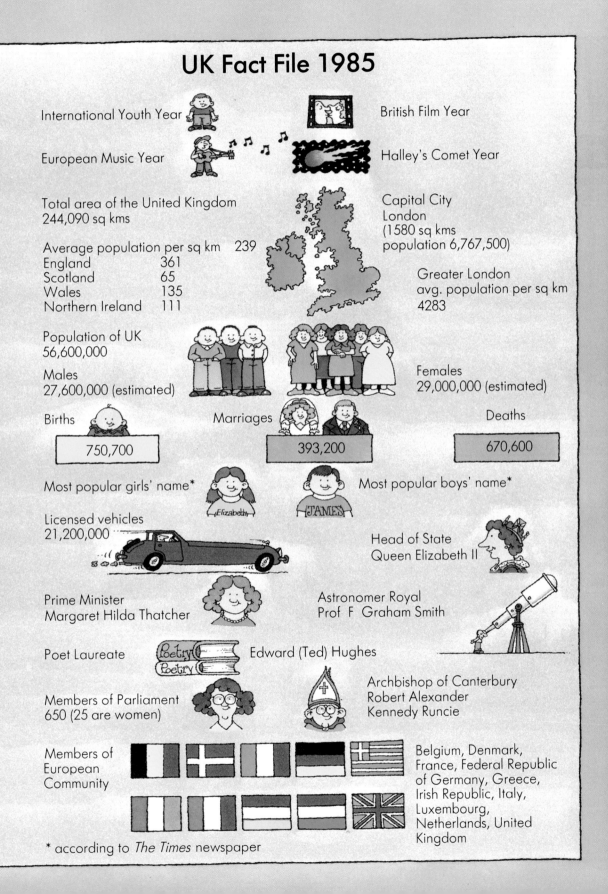

International Youth Year

British Film Year

European Music Year

Halley's Comet Year

Total area of the United Kingdom
244,090 sq kms

Capital City
London
(1580 sq kms
population 6,767,500)

Average population per sq km    239
England            361
Scotland           65
Wales              135
Northern Ireland   111

Greater London
avg. population per sq km
4283

Population of UK
56,600,000

Males
27,600,000 (estimated)

Females
29,000,000 (estimated)

Births

Marriages

Deaths

750,700

393,200

670,600

Most popular girls' name*

*Elizabeth*

*JAMES*

Most popular boys' name*

Licensed vehicles
21,200,000

Head of State
Queen Elizabeth II

Prime Minister
Margaret Hilda Thatcher

Astronomer Royal
Prof F Graham Smith

Poet Laureate    Poetry Poetry    Edward (Ted) Hughes

Members of Parliament
650 (25 are women)

Archbishop of Canterbury
Robert Alexander
Kennedy Runcie

Members of
European
Community

Belgium, Denmark,
France, Federal Republic
of Germany, Greece,
Irish Republic, Italy,
Luxembourg,
Netherlands, United
Kingdom

* according to *The Times* newspaper

# March

**Friday March 1**
St David's Day. The Prince of Wales is the first Royal Blood Donor! He gives a pint of blood (O Rhesus Negative) at the North London Transfusion Centre. Rain and snow in the Midlands.

**Saturday March 2**
A rare Little Crake, a small brown semi-wader from Eastern Europe, arrives at the Seven Sisters Country Park, nr Seaford, Sussex. Rain and snow in the West.

**Sunday March 3**
A 13.7m sperm whale is washed up on the beach near Skegness, Lincolnshire. 49mm of rain at Trawsfynydd, Gwynedd. Gales in the West.

**Monday March 4**
South-west England is on flood alert because of freak high tides: thousands of sand bags are distributed.

**Tuesday March 5**
Four schoolgirls from Ashford, Kent, win a competition to send a scientific experiment into space. Their crystal-growing entry will be tested on board a NASA space shuttle next year.

**Wednesday March 6**
Ivan Lawrence, Conservative MP for Burton-on-Trent, talks for 4hrs 23mins in the House of Commons about the fluoridation of water: the longest speech this century!

**Thursday March 7**
Mons Meg, a huge medieval cannon from Edinburgh, goes on display at the Tower of London.

Full Moon

**Friday March 8**
4500-tonne nuclear submarine *HMS Torbay* is launched at Barrow-in-Furness. Tower Bridge, London, closes tonight until 6am on Monday for painting.

**Saturday March 9**
Peter Duncan, from BBC TV's 'Blue Peter', sets off from Portpatrick, Wigtownshire, to drive across the Irish Sea in a converted VW Beetle. He breaks down and has to be towed to Bangor by boat.

**Sunday March 10**
Mount Etna in Sicily erupts: a stream of molten lava, more than 900m long, pours from the south-east crater.

**Monday March 11**
Commonwealth Day. The Al-Fayed brothers buy Harrods in London. Mikhail Gorbachev (54) is named as the new General Secretary of the Soviet Communist Party.

**Tuesday March 12**
The Queen is to get a new armoured train with bullet-proof windows.

# *March*

Named after the Roman god Mars. It has also been known as 'rough month', 'lengthening month', 'boisterous month' and 'windy month'.

## Seeds in Time

The time capsule buried on March 22 in the foundations of the new tropical conservatory at Kew Gardens is a glass ball just over 38cm in diameter. In it there are dried seeds of basic crops and endangered species from Kew Seed Bank, sealed in special glass vials. There are also some books and reports on the subject. The seeds include *Oryza sativa* (rice), *Pisum sativum* (garden pea), *Leonurus cardiaca* (motherwort), *Saintpaulia* (African violet), *Primula veris* (cowslip), *Dianthus gratianopolitanus* (Cheddar pink) and *Hyacinthoides non-scripta* (bluebell).

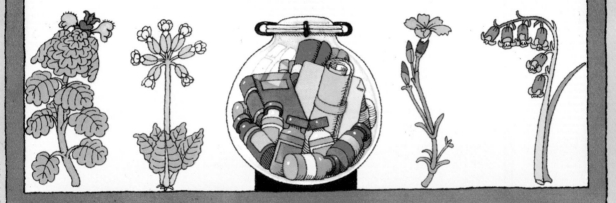

**March 12:** Post Office issues new insect stamps to mark the centenaries of the Royal Entomological Society of London's Royal Charter, and the Selborne Society.

17p Buff Tailed Bumble Bee — 22p Seven Spotted Ladybird — 29p Wart-Biter Bush-Cricket — 31p Stag Beetle — 34p Emperor Dragonfly

| | |
|---|---|
| *Wednesday*<br>*March 13* | Martin Moran (30), from Sheffield, arrives in Fort William after climbing all the Munro Peaks in Scotland in 83 days. There are 277 peaks and they are all over 900m high. |
| *Thursday*<br>*March 14* | Pentonville Road Park, in Islington, London, is to be called Grimaldi Park—after the famous 19th-century clown, Joseph Grimaldi, who is buried there. |
| *Friday*<br>*March 15* | 10,000 NATO troops test their Arctic warfare skills in military exercises in Norway. Heavy snow falls in the north of England and Scotland. |
| *Saturday*<br>*March 16* | More than 20cm of snow falls in Lincolnshire tonight and a freak storm cuts off Grantham. Snowdrifts in Scotland. |
| *Sunday*<br>*March 17* | St Patrick's Day. Libby Riddles (28), from Teller, Alaska, becomes the first woman to win the 1688km Iditarod Trail dog sledge race from Anchorage to Nome. They cover the distance in 17 days 20mins 17secs. |
| *Monday*<br>*March 18* | Four soldiers from the Royal Green Jackets end a 29-day expedition retracing Lawrence of Arabia's 1000km camel trail across the desert. They lived like Bedouins, cooking bread over thorn fires and sleeping in tents of woven goat hair. |
| *Tuesday*<br>*March 19* | Budget Day; petrol goes up by 4p to just over £2 a gallon. |
| *Wednesday*<br>*March 20* | First day of spring! Snow showers along the east coast, from Kent to Scotland. Part of Poole Quay in Dorset is sealed off while bomb experts explode a 25cm shell found off the Isle of Wight. |
| *Thursday*<br>*March 21* | British and French governments give their approval for a Channel tunnel or bridge. A BR Inter-City 125 breaks the rail speed record between Paddington and Plymouth, covering the 363.15km in 2hrs 31mins 44secs.<br><br>New Moon |
| *Friday*<br>*March 22* | David Attenborough buries a time capsule in the foundations of the new tropical conservatory at the Royal Botanical Gardens, Kew. |
| *Saturday*<br>*March 23* | Seven of the 10 red squirrels released in Regent's Park, London, last October and November have survived the winter. One was killed by a car, one by a feral cat and another disappeared after its radio collar failed. |

| | |
|---|---|
| *Sunday*<br>*March 24* | Zola Budd wins the first world women's cross-country championship in Lisbon. She runs the 4860m barefoot in 15mins 0.1sec. |
| *Monday*<br>*March 25* | A 'letter of peace', 566.3m long, written by more than 1000 American children, is delivered to the US arms delegation in Geneva. |
| *Tuesday*<br>*March 26* | Scaffolding is put up around the Devil's Chimney, a huge, crumbling rock near Cheltenham, Gloucs. Steel rods are drilled into it to stop it moving. |
| *Wednesday*<br>*March 27* | A pair of golden eagles have returned to their breeding site in the Lake District and are guarded day and night by RSPB patrols. |
| *Thursday*<br>*March 28* | Concorde flies 9654km from London to Cape Town in 8hrs 8mins—3hrs faster than the previous record, set in 1977. |

Maximum temperature at Lerwick, Shetlands -1.6°C.

| | |
|---|---|
| *Friday*<br>*March 29* | The Nature Conservancy Council launches a nationwide search for the Crested Warty Newt (*Triturus Cristatus*). |
| *Saturday*<br>*March 30* | *Last Suspect* (50–1 outsider), from Letcombe Bassett in Berkshire, wins the Grand National at Aintree. Maximum temperature at Finningley, Yorkshire, 17.1°C. |
| *Sunday*<br>*March 31* | Summer Time begins at 1am—clocks go forward 1hr. *The Royal Scotsman* steams into Marylebone Station, London, to be refitted for luxury tours of the Scottish Highlands. |

### Budget Day

Budget comes from the old French word *bougette*, which means little bag. The Chancellor of the Exchequer's little bag, which carries all his important budget papers, is, in fact, a 125-year-old wooden box. It was made for W E Gladstone, who was Chancellor between 1852 and 1882. It is covered in red leather and you can still see Queen Victoria's gold monogram and the words Chancellor of Exchequer on it.

| The Universe | Nosy Parker | Daily Gossip | The Frog |
|---|---|---|---|
| DOGS GET FREE TRAVEL ON LONDON BUSES AND TUBE TRAINS | PRODUCTION OF THE SINCLAIR C5 ELECTRIC TRICYCLE SUSPENDED | FOOTBALL FANS RAMPAGE THROUGH LUTON | NATIONAL UNION OF MINEWORKERS CALL OFF YEAR-LONG STRIKE |

# April

| | |
|---|---|
| *Monday*<br>*April 1* | The remains of a 150,000,000-year-old crocodile have been found at a claypit near Peterborough, Cambs. |
| *Tuesday*<br>*April 2* | Hans Christian Andersen was born in 1805. Launch of British Film Year in London. |
| *Wednesday*<br>*April 3* | Princess Michael of Kent opens the 50th Happy Eater restaurant by the A3 at Wisley, nr Guildford, Surrey. |
| *Thursday*<br>*April 4* | The Queen presents Royal Maundy Money to 59 women and 59 men at Ripon Cathedral, Yorkshire. Each person is given silver Maundy pence to the value of 59p—equal to the Queen's age. |
| *Friday*<br>*April 5* | Good Friday. 64km traffic jam on M1 from Junction 13 at Milton Keynes to Junction 18 at Rugby. Full Moon |
| *Saturday*<br>*April 6* | First day of Passover. 131st University Boat Race: Oxford wins by 4¾ lengths. Good day for the Severn Bore, the tidal wave that runs for 32km along the Severn below Gloucester, when tides are especially high. |
| *Sunday*<br>*April 7* | Easter Sunday. The pop group Wham! sing to an audience of 10,000 in the Workers' Gymnasium, Peking. |
| *Monday*<br>*April 8* | Bank Holiday. A 6m whale is washed up on the beach at Pett, between Rye and Hastings. Mark Ryder (24), from Tuffley, Gloucs, eats 1000 baby eels in 21secs to win the world elver-eating championship for the third year running. |
| *Tuesday*<br>*April 9* | Nipper, a Border Collie, is presented with the RSPCA's top award for animal bravery, the Plaque for Intelligence and Courage, for saving a flock of 300 sheep from a fire. |
| *Wednesday*<br>*April 10* | Countdown begins for the launch of the US space shuttle *Discovery* at Cape Canaveral in 2 days' time. |

50.5mm of rain falls at Nantmor, Gwynedd.

| | |
|---|---|
| *Thursday*<br>*April 11* | A fire has been raging on Isabela in the Galapagos Islands for the past 6 weeks. It has devastated 40,000 hectares and endangered the giant Galapagos tortoise and the rare dark-rumped Petrel. |
| *Friday*<br>*April 12* | The US space shuttle *Discovery* is launched successfully from Cape Canaveral at 8.59 local time, after being postponed 5 times. The crew includes Senator Jack Garn—the first civilian observer in space. |

| | |
|---|---|
| *Saturday*<br>*April 13* | Pottery from the wreck of an early 16th-century Spanish trading ship, discovered in Studland Bay, Dorset, last year goes on display in Poole. |
| *Sunday*<br>*April 14* | Robin Knox-Johnston (45) sails into Plymouth after sailing across the Atlantic in 10 days 14hrs 18mins in his 18.3m catamaran—a new British record. |
| *Monday*<br>*April 15* | Glen Sutcliffe (22), from Blaydon, Tyne and Wear, and Jill Channing (21), from Stockton-on-Tees, leave Tynemouth Haven to canoe round Britain. |
| *Tuesday*<br>*April 16* | Two shuttle astronauts go on a 3-hr space walk. They attach tools that look like fly swatters to the end of *Discovery's* robot arm in an attempt to rescue a satellite that failed to go into orbit on Saturday. |
| *Wednesday*<br>*April 17* | Zara the giraffe (11 months), who is 3.6m tall and weighs over 380kg, travels from London Zoo to Chessington, avoiding low bridges and overhead cables. The journey takes 2hrs. |

# *April*

The opening month—from the Latin 'aperire', which means to open. Also known as the time of budding.

# British Bores

When there are very high tides—especially at the equinoxes—the Severn Bore runs like a tidal wave along the river below Gloucester, travelling at nearly 20kph and reaching heights of 3m. (There is an annual kayak race along it in September from Newnham to Minsterworth.) There are other (smaller) British bores on the Yorkshire Ouse and the Trent, but they are known as eagres—from the Scandinavian name for waves.

## Scoop
LONDON, BIRMINGHAM AND MANCHESTER BID FOR OLYMPICS

## Grapevine
CHRIS BONINGTON REACHES SUMMIT OF MT EVEREST

## Daily Blurb
REMAINS OF PREHISTORIC WOOLLY MAMMOTH FOUND IN NORFOLK

## Daily Chatter
ANTI-NUCLEAR DEMONSTRATIONS AT MOLESWORTH, CAMBS

| | |
|---|---|
| *Thursday*<br>*April 18* | The Gloucestershire Naturalists' Society launches a survey of the glow-worm population. |
| *Friday*<br>*April 19* | The US space shuttle *Discovery* arrives back at Cape Canaveral 90mins late because of rain! New Moon |
| *Saturday*<br>*April 20* | Yellow ten shilling notes and green £1 notes, made for the Stannary Parliament, go on sale in Cornwall. They mark the birthday of the famous railway pioneer Richard Trevithick. |
| *Sunday*<br>*April 21* | The 5th London Marathon at 9.30am. By 3pm, 16,000 competitors have crossed the finishing line. Steve Jones (29) from Wales wins in 2hr 8mins 16secs, and Ingrid Kristiansen (29), Norway, sets a women's world record in 2hrs 21mins 6secs. |
| *Monday*<br>*April 22* | Traffic lights will be put on a motorway for the first time at Junction 10 on the M6, north of Birmingham. |
| *Tuesday*<br>*April 23* | St George's Day. Coca-Cola announces that it is going to change its flavour—for the first time in 99 years! |
| *Wednesday*<br>*April 24* | Britain's first Sikh woman magistrate, Mrs Ajeet Harbans Singh, is sworn in at Southwark Crown Court in London. |
| *Thursday*<br>*April 25* | The Nature Conservancy Council announces 3 new nature reserves in Scotland—Dunnet Links and Blar nam Faoileag in Caithness, and at Cragbank Woods in the Borders. |
| *Friday*<br>*April 26* | Greenpeace demonstrators slide down the front of Harrods on ropes and unfurl a banner saying STOP FUR SHAME. |
| *Saturday*<br>*April 27* | Flu epidemic in Staffordshire. Icy winds from the Arctic bring snow and hail. During one of these showers, the temperature in London falls by nearly 6° to only 3°C. |
| *Sunday*<br>*April 28* | The hovercraft *Princess Anne* is damaged by a freak wave in the Channel on her way back from Calais to Dover. |
| *Monday*<br>*April 29* | The US space shuttle *Challenger* is launched from the Kennedy Space Center in Florida on a week-long scientific mission. Emperor Hirohito of Japan is 84. |
| *Tuesday*<br>*April 30* | The Venerable Wilfred Wood, Archdeacon of Southwark, is appointed Suffragan Bishop of Croydon: he is the first black bishop in the Church of England. |

# Top Tens of The Year 1985

*Top Ten Singles*
compiled by Gallup for BPI

1. The Power of Love (Jennifer Rush)
2. I Know Him So Well (Elaine Paige & Barbara Dickson)
3. Into The Groove (Madonna)
4. 19 (Paul Hardcastle)
5. Frankie (Sister Sledge)
6. Dancing In The Street (David Bowie & Mick Jagger)
7. Move Closer (Phyllis Nelson)
8. A Good Heart (Fergal Sharkey)
9. Take On Me (A-Ha)
10. Love and Pride (King)

© BPI

*Top Ten Historic Properties and Gardens 1985*
according to the British Tourist Authority

1. Tower of London (2,430,323 visitors)
2. Royal Botanical Gardens, Kew (1,112,177 visitors)
3. Roman Baths, Bath (989,382 visitors)
4. Edinburgh Castle (923,256 visitors)
5. Royal Botanical Gardens, Edinburgh (820,387 visitors)
6. Windsor Castle (735,000 visitors)
7. Stonehenge (655,690 visitors)
8. Warwick Castle (640,919 visitors)
9. Hampton Court Palace (614,929 visitors)
10. Beaulieu, Hants (551,879 visitors)

# What to do with a dead whale

Dead whales that are washed up on British beaches count as wrecks.
They have to be reported to the Receiver of Wreck and a special WRE5
form is filled in, according to Part 9 of the Merchant Shipping Act 1894.
The Receiver then has to make arrangements to dispose of the body,
either by burying it or by towing it back out to sea and sinking it with the
help of a lot of scrap metal.

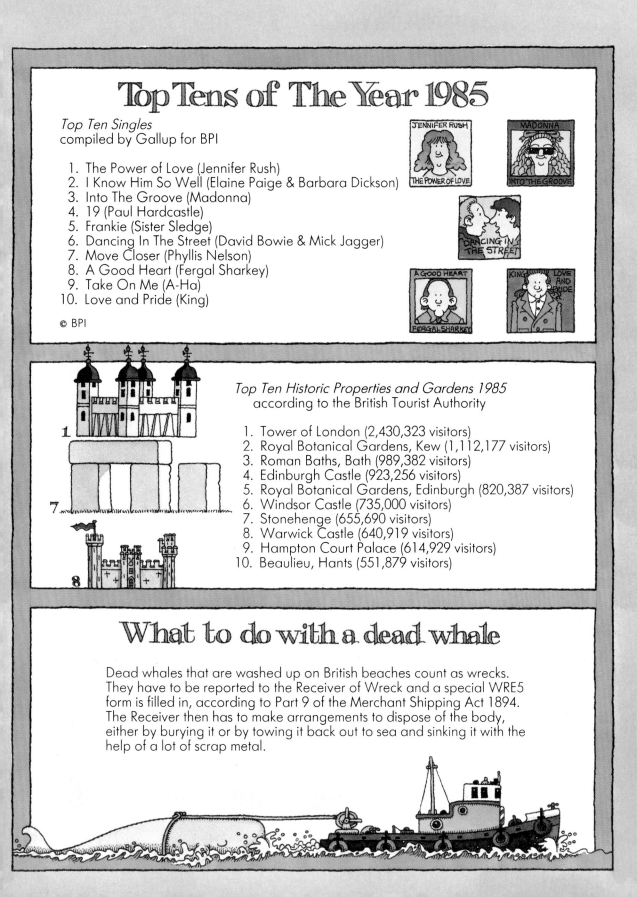

# May

| | |
|---|---|
| *Wednesday*<br>*May 1* | May Day. A baby camel is born at London Zoo to Anya and Archie. She weighs 22.7kg and is called May! |
| *Thursday*<br>*May 2* | Special medals are being made to commemorate the 40th anniversary of VE Day. There will be a limited edition of 50 gold (£1035 each), 500 silver (£97.75 each) and 5,000 bronze (£22.50 each). |
| *Friday*<br>*May 3* | British driving licences will change from green to pink next year to be the same as the rest of the EEC. |
| *Saturday*<br>*May 4* | A rare eclipse of the moon takes place at 8.22pm. Eurovision Song Contest in Gothenburg, Sweden. Norway wins, Germany comes second, Sweden 3rd and Britain 4th. |
| *Sunday*<br>*May 5* | Ian Meadows (29), from Leicester, wins BBC's 'Mastermind' title. He answers specialized questions on the English Civil War. |
| *Monday*<br>*May 6* | Bank Holiday. Maura O'Boyle wins the Belfast City Women's Marathon in 2hrs 45mins 40secs and Marty Deane wins the Men's in 2hrs 15mins 51secs. |
| *Tuesday*<br>*May 7* | Princess Michael of Kent launches *Virgin Atlantic Challenger* at Hamble. The 19.8m catamaran has two 1200 horse-power engines and will try to break the record for crossing the Atlantic later this summer. |
| *Wednesday*<br>*May 8* | 40th Anniversary of VE Day. The flag that covered Nelson's body at Trafalgar is sold for £8,000 in London. |

33mm of rain at Whitby, Yorkshire

| | |
|---|---|
| *Thursday*<br>*May 9* | Launch of National Bike Week. London Zoo announces a £21,000,000 redevelopment plan. |
| *Friday*<br>*May 10* | Col John Blashford-Snell, a director of the 4-year round-the-world adventure Operation Raleigh, says that the expedition has found the remains of the legendary lost White City (Ciudad Blanca) in Honduras. |
| *Saturday*<br>*May 11* | Cat Fancy Supreme Show starts at the National Exhibition Centre, Birmingham. Biggin Hill Air Fair celebrates 40yrs of jet aviation. |
| *Sunday*<br>*May 12* | Prince Andrew opens the new airport at Mount Pleasant on the Falkland Islands. |

# *May*

Takes its name from Maia, the goddess of growth and increase, or from 'maiores', the Latin word for elders, who were honoured this month.

The Anglo Saxons called it 'thrimilce' because cows could be milked three times a day now.

An old Dutch name was 'bloumaand', which means blossoming month.

## Star Pavement

To celebrate British Film Year, famous film stars leave their handprints in wet cement on a special new Star Pavement in Leicester Square, London, this month. This year, visits to the cinema go up by more than a third to about 64,000,000. Altogether, there are 1310 cinema screens in the country. The Top Ten films of the year are:

1. Ghostbusters
2. View To A Kill
3. Gremlins
4. Rambo First Blood—Part II
5. Beverly Hills Cop
6. Police Academy II—Their First Assignment
7. Santa Claus The Movie
8. A Passage To India
9. 101 Dalmatians
10. Desperately Seeking Susan

© *Screen International*

**Daily Octopus**

FIRE SWEEPS THROUGH BRADFORD CITY FOOTBALL GROUND

**Trumpet**

MORE THAN 40 PEOPLE DIE IN FOOTBALL RIOTS AT HEYSAL STADIUM IN BRUSSELS AT THE EUROPEAN CUP FINAL

**The Herald**

A GOLDEN EAGLE EGG HATCHES IN THE LAKE DISTRICT

**Newsreel**

LEGIONNAIRE'S DISEASE IN STAFFORDSHIRE

BR TO INSTALL INTERCITY TELEPHONES

| | |
|---|---|
| *Monday*<br>*May 13* | The scaffolding which has hidden Big Ben's clock tower in London since August 1983 starts to come down. |
| *Tuesday*<br>*May 14* | Inauguration of the Peace Pagoda in Battersea Park, London. It's 33.5m high and took the monks from the Japanese Nipponzan Myohji Buddhist sect 10 months to build—with a little help from London Community Builders. |

39mm of rain at Leeming, Yorkshire

| | |
|---|---|
| *Wednesday*<br>*May 15* | Conservationists occupy a meadow in Mersea Island, Essex, to try to save a colony of rare wild green-winged orchids from the builder's bulldozer. |
| *Thursday*<br>*May 16* | The Spa Fountain in the Pump Room, Bath, is turned on again for the first time since an amoeba contaminated the water 7 years ago. It costs 25p a glass. |
| *Friday*<br>*May 17* | *RRS Discovery*, which took Capt Scott to the Antarctic at the beginning of the century, is re-rigged in St Katherine's Dock, London. Temperatures reach 23°C in Hampshire. |
| *Saturday*<br>*May 18* | Manchester United beats Everton 1–0 to win the Cup Final. Kevin Moran (Manchester United) becomes the first player in the history of the FA Cup Final to be sent off. |
| *Sunday*<br>*May 19* | The worst forest fires ever in Florida: more than 40,000 hectares and 200 homes are destroyed. 48.6kg thresher shark is caught near the Nab Tower off the Isle of Wight by Brian Rogers, from Hounslow. |

New Moon

| | |
|---|---|
| *Monday*<br>*May 20* | Campaign to stamp out Giant Japanese Seaweed starts behind Chesil Beach in Dorset. Snorkel divers will remove the weed from the sea bed. |
| *Tuesday*<br>*May 21* | Mohammed Ajeeb (47) becomes Britain's first Asian Lord Mayor in Bradford. A teddy bear in a white dress is sold for £2090 at Sotheby's auction rooms in London. |
| *Wednesday*<br>*May 22* | There is a new hovercraft service across the Bristol Channel. The first trip is between Barry, Glam, and Burnham-on-Sea, Somerset. |
| *Thursday*<br>*May 23* | The RAF Red Devils parachute into the gardens of Kensington Palace, London, to launch their appeal for a new aircraft. Inauguration of a new nature reserve off the Falkland Islands, where albatross, skua and penguins nest and sea-lions and elephant seals breed. |

| | |
|---|---|
| *Friday*<br>*May 24* | Pogo the pelican is fitted with an artificial glass fibre leg at Chessington Zoo. David Edwards (38), from Stoke-on-Trent, wins Mensa's Superbrain of Britain competition. |
| *Saturday*<br>*May 25* | Queen Regent Ntombi of Swaziland drops her last name (which means 'girl') and will now be called Indlovukazi of Swaziland. |
| *Sunday*<br>*May 26* | Whit Sunday. Mrs Helena Sanders (74), from Truro, Cornwall, is made a Cavalieri di San Marco (a Knight of St Mark) after spending 20 years looking after stray cats in Venice. |
| *Monday*<br>*May 27* | Bank Holiday. A needle-tailed swift, last seen in England in 1879, spends 2 hours at the Fairburn Ings nature reserve near Leeds. |
| *Tuesday*<br>*May 28* | Urban Wildlife Week in Birmingham. Operation Kingfisher is launched to lure kingfishers back to the river Cole. |
| *Wednesday*<br>*May 29* | The world's first nuclear-powered submarine, the *US Nautilus*, launched in 1954, leaves San Francisco. It is towed to New London, Connecticut, to become a floating museum. |
| *Thursday*<br>*May 30* | The Duke of Edinburgh leads a procession of horse-drawn carriages 4.7km across Morecambe Sands, Cumbria, from Silverdale to Grange-over-Sands. It's the first safe crossing for 100 years! |
| *Friday*<br>*May 31* | A tornado devastates the north-east of the United States and Canada. |

### The Weather in May

**May 3:** Minimum temperature at St Harmon, Powys, −4.6°C, maximum temperature at Binbrook, Lincs, 5.1°C.
**May 20:** 58.1mm of rain at Brize Norton, Oxon.
**May 26:** Torrential rain and storms. Hailstones and 70kph winds devastate crops in Essex. Floods in the west country.

**May 14:** The Post Office issues 4 new Europa stamps to celebrate European Music Year.

THIRTY·ONE·PENCE

THE·FIRST·CUCKOO
*Frederick Delius*

SEVENTEEN·PENCE

WATER·MUSIC
*George Frideric Handel*

TWENTY·TWO·PENCE

THE·PLANETS·SUITE
*Gustav Holst*

THIRTY·FOUR·PENCE

SEA·PICTURES
*Edward Elgar*

# June

**Saturday June 1**
Scuttlebrook Wake at Chipping Campden, Gloucs. Mrs Evelyn Slack wins the Harness Racing Derby at Green Hammerton, near York.

**Sunday June 2**
Veteran cars parade through Coventry to mark the opening of the World Motoring Centenary. Mrs Anne Williams, of Swansea, is 112 today.

**Monday June 3**
PC Gil Boyd, from Cambridge, raises £10,000 for Great Ormond Street Children's Hospital by abseiling 147.5m down the Telecom tower in London. It takes just under 4 mins! Full Moon

**Tuesday June 4**
It's so hot that the tarmac melts for 1.6km between Totnes and Buckfastleigh, Devon.

**Wednesday June 5**
*Slip Anchor*, the 9–4 favourite ridden by Steven Cauthen, wins the Derby at Epsom by 7 lengths. 51.6mm of rain at Hadley, Hereford and Worcester.

**Thursday June 6**
50 protected Great Crested Newts are rescued from a farmer's pond at Newhall, Derbyshire.

**Friday June 7**
A plaque is unveiled on a windmill at Snape, Suffolk, where Benjamin Britten wrote most of his music. It marks the 40th anniversary of the first performance of his opera 'Peter Grimes'.

**Saturday June 8**
Featherweight boxer Barry McGuigan (N. Ireland) beats Eusebio Pedroza (Panama) in the world championship at Queen's Park Rangers' football ground in London.

**Sunday June 9**
Two Soviet cosmonauts, Vladimir Dzhanibekov and Viktor Savinykh, dock their T-13 space capsule with the orbiting space station Salyut-7 which has been empty for 7 months. It's the first manual docking ever!

**Monday June 10**
The Honourable Artillery Company fires a 62-gun salute from the Tower of London to wish the Duke of Edinburgh a happy 64th birthday.

**Tuesday June 11**
US scientists at the Jet Propulsion Lab in Pasadena pick up signals from the Soviet space probe, launched last December, that has just landed on the surface of Venus. A Fabergé egg is sold in New York for £1,375,000.

**Wednesday June 12**
A BR locomotive is named *The Times* in a ceremony at Euston Station to celebrate the newspaper's 200th birthday.

# June

Takes its name from the great goddess Juno, or from 'juniores', the Latin word for young people, who were honoured this month.

The old Dutch name was 'Zomer-maand', which means summer month.

The old Saxon name was 'Sere-monath', which means dry month.

## Prince Sultan bin Salman ibn Abdul Aziz al-Saud, Astronaut

On June 17 US space shuttle *Discovery* blasts off from Cape Canaveral at 7.33am local time (12.33BST). On board is the first Arab astronaut, Prince Sultan bin Salman ibn Abdul Aziz al-Saud, nephew of King Fahd of Saudi Arabia. He has received special permission to pray on board without the usual ritual washings and will observe the new moon, which marks the end of Ramadan, the Muslim month of fasting.

**June 8:** Adder warning in the West Country because of the mild weather

**June 18:** The Post Office issues four new 'Safety at Sea' stamps

*The Million Pound Egg*
The gold and enamel Fabergé egg, sold this month for £1,375,000, is 20cm high and was made for Tsar Nicholas II in 1900. It has a clock face on it with diamond numbers and a golden rooster on the top, which flaps its wings and crows. Peter Carl Fabergé, a famous goldsmith, was born in St Petersburg in 1846 and made the first of his imperial Easter eggs for Tsar Alexander III in 1885. Altogether he made 54.

| | |
|---|---|
| *Thursday*<br>*June 13* | A gold penny from the reign of Henry III, dated 1257, is sold for £65,000 at Spinks in London. |
| *Friday*<br>*June 14* | The Queen unveils a memorial in the crypt of St Paul's Cathedral to the 255 men who died in the Falklands War in 1982. |
| *Saturday*<br>*June 15* | Earth tremors in southern Sweden and the Danish island of Zeeland measure 4.5 on the Richter Scale. The Queen's official birthday: she rides 'Burmese' for the 17th time at the Trooping the Colour. |
| *Sunday*<br>*June 16* | Father's Day. The oil tanker *Bridgeness* runs aground off West Wales, causing an oil slick more than 6km long nr Grassholm Island. |
| *Monday*<br>*June 17* | US space shuttle *Discovery* blasts off from Cape Canaveral at 7.33am local time (12.33BST) with the first Arab astronaut on board. He is Prince Sultan Salman al-Saud, of Saudi Arabia, King Fahd's nephew. |
| *Tuesday*<br>*June 18* | Johnny Morris and Sharron Davies launch 'Project Zambia', a World Wildlife Fund appeal against elephant poaching in Zambia.<br><br>New Moon |
| *Wednesday*<br>*June 19* | A clutch of white-headed ducks' eggs is flown from the Wildfowl Trust at Slimbridge, Gloucs, to Hungary to help save the ducks from extinction. They came from Eastern Europe originally. |
| *Thursday*<br>*June 20* | Ruth Lawrence (13), from Huddersfield, takes the first paper in her Maths Finals at Oxford University—a year early! |
| *Friday*<br>*June 21* | The Longest Day. Stonehenge is closed so Druids can't perform their special summer solstice ceremony there. Prince William is 3! |
| *Saturday*<br>*June 22* | European Music Day. The 8 men and 1 woman who are paddling across the Indian Ocean from SE Asia to Madagascar in a giant canoe put into the Cocos Is. They've sprung a leak. |
| *Sunday*<br>*June 23* | King Fahd of Saudi Arabia telephones his nephew on board the US space shuttle *Discovery*. |
| *Monday*<br>*June 24* | Midsummer's Day. Play is postponed on the opening day of the 99th Wimbledon Lawn Tennis Championships because of torrential rain. Lightning strikes a new building next to the Centre Court. |

| | |
|---|---|
| *Tuesday* *June 25* | A bat population survey is carried out in London by the Fauna and Flora Preservation Society. 42 competitors set off on the 320km, 5 day Solar-mobile race from Zurich, Switzerland. |
| *Wednesday* *June 26* | The United Nations is 40. Mass whale-beaching in New South Wales, Australia. Trawlers tow 21 stranded whales to safety from Crowdy Head. |
| *Thursday* *June 27* | Freak winds up to 345,600kph from the Sun batter Halley's Comet, which is approaching the inner solar system at nearly 80,000kph. |
| *Friday* *June 28* | The Torquay–Channel Islands hydrofoil hits a shark and has its engines torn out. |
| *Saturday* *June 29* | Inauguration of the British Sir Isaac Newton telescope on La Palma in the Canaries. It will be the 3rd most powerful optical telescope in the world. |

> The Beatles' psychedelic Rolls Royce is sold for £1,768,462 in New York.

| | |
|---|---|
| *Sunday* *June 30* | One 'leap second' is subtracted from clocks at midnight GMT to make up for the slight irregularity of the Earth's rotation. |

# Family 1985

On average, each member of Family 1985 drinks 2.3 litres of milk each week and eats 110.8 grams of cheese, 1kg 42 grams of meat, 138.9 grams of fish, 3.15 eggs, 285.4 grams of fat and oil, 281.1 grams of sugar, 3kg 174 grams of fruit and vegetables and 1kg 526 grams of cereals (including bread).

(These figures are taken from the National Food Survey)

*Weekly Shopping Bill for One*

| | |
|---|---|
| Milk and cream | 98.66p |
| Cheese | 31.32p |
| Meat | 273.51p |
| Fish | 44.54p |
| Eggs | 21.10p |
| Fats and oils | 36.77p |
| Sugar and preserves | 17.36p |
| Fruit & vegetables | 173.43p |
| Cereals (including bread) | 144.12p |
| *Total* | 840.81p (£8.41) |

# July

| | |
|---|---|
| *Monday*<br>*July 1* | Canada Day. The Princess of Wales is 24 today. A team of 20 divers finishes a 2-week exploration of the *Stirling Castle*, which sank in November 1703 on the Goodwin Sands off Deal, Kent. |
| *Tuesday*<br>*July 2* | An Ariane rocket carrying the European Space Agency's *Giotto* spacecraft lifts off from French Guiana. *Giotto* will intercept Halley's Comet next March.　　　　　Full Moon |
| *Wednesday*<br>*July 3* | A cricket match between Hertfordshire and Worcestershire at Hitchin, Herts, is interrupted by a swarm of bees. |
| *Thursday*<br>*July 4* | Ruth Lawrence (13) from Huddersfield, is awarded a first class honours degree in maths at Oxford. |
| *Friday*<br>*July 5* | RSPB say that about 5,000 seabirds, including a colony of puffins, have died around the coast of south-west Wales because of oil spilling from the grounded tanker *Bridgeness*. |

3.8mm of rain falls in 20mins at Wimbledon.

| | |
|---|---|
| *Saturday*<br>*July 6* | Martina Navratilova beats Chris Lloyd 4–6, 6–3, 6–2, in the Women's Finals at the Wimbledon Lawn Tennis Championships. |
| *Sunday*<br>*July 7* | Boris Becker (17) beats Kevin Curren 6–3, 6–7, 7–6, 6–4, to become the first unseeded Men's Champion at Wimbledon. He's the youngest winner ever. |
| *Monday*<br>*July 8* | The rare Heath Fritillary is breeding again in Essex after an absence of 15yrs—according to the Essex Naturalists' Trust. |
| *Tuesday*<br>*July 9* | Divers discover gold, silver and jewellery, worth about £4,000,000, in the wreck of the *Royal Charles*, which sank off Anglesey in 1859 on its way back from Australia. |
| *Wednesday*<br>*July 10* | Coca-Cola announce that they are going to bring back the old flavour that they replaced in the spring. They will call it Coca-Cola Classic. |
| *Thursday*<br>*July 11* | *The Times* newspaper celebrates its 200th birthday with a party at Hampton Court Palace. |
| *Friday*<br>*July 12* | Harrods takes £5,200,000 on the first day of the summer sale. The US space shuttle *Challenger*'s launch is called off 3secs before lift-off! |
| *Saturday*<br>*July 13* | One and a half billion people in 160 countries watch the Live Aid concert at Wembley Stadium on television. It raises over £50,000,000 for starving people in Africa. |

# July

## The Stirling Castle

The 1087 ton, 70 gun *Stirling Castle* went down in the Great Storm which devastated southern England on Nov 26 and 27, 1703. Thousands of people died during the storm, both at sea and on land. Four large naval vessels went down on the Goodwin Sands, off Deal, Kent, including the *Stirling Castle*. The wrecks were discovered late in 1979 and, since then, hundreds of objects have been brought up by divers. They include cannons, muskets, ship's kettles, thimbles, microscopes, swords, scrubbing brushes, sand-glasses, dark green 'onion' bottles, china cups, toothbrushes, leather shoes, combs and razors! Everything will go on show at the Ramsgate Maritime Museum.

Illustrations are based on articles and drawings supplied by Thanet Archaeological Society.

**July 30:** The Royal Mail is 350 years old

17ᴾ ROYAL MAIL · 350 YEARS OF SERVICE

22ᴾ ROYAL MAIL · 350 YEARS OF SERVICE

31ᴾ ROYAL MAIL · 350 YEARS OF SERVICE

34ᴾ ROYAL MAIL · 350 YEARS OF SERVICE

**Reporter**
TRUCE IN SPAGHETTI WAR BETWEEN EEC AND US: HIGH TARIFFS ON EEC PASTA AND US LEMONS AND WALNUTS SUSPENDED

**DAILY BEACON**
TOXIC ANTI-FREEZE FOUND IN AUSTRIAN WINE

**The Herald**
GREATER LONDON COUNCIL AND METROPOLITAN COUNTIES ARE ABOLISHED

**Chit-Chat**
HOMO SAPIENS URBANUS GOES ON SHOW AT LONDON ZOO: HE EATS, WASHES, SHAVES, READS NEWSPAPERS AND WATCHES TV

**July 26:** The Soviet research ship *Mikhail Somov* is freed today after 133 days trapped in Antarctic ice.

| | |
|---|---|
| *Sunday*<br>*July 14* | Mrs Helen Fraser (38), from Chester, wins the first British Trivial Pursuits Championship. |
| *Monday*<br>*July 15* | St Swithin's Day. Sammy, a 6-month-old seal, is stranded over 80km inland on a mud bank near Thorpe Marsh power station in Doncaster. |
| *Tuesday*<br>*July 16* | Steve Cram, from Gateshead, breaks Steve Ovett's 1983 1500m world record in Nice. His time is 3mins 29.67secs. Sammy the seal is taken to a special seal sanctuary in King's Lynn until he's well enough to go back to sea. |
| *Wednesday*<br>*July 17* | Argentine fruit goes on sale for the first time since the Falklands War: Red Delicious apples are 40p per lb. A gust of wind measures 101.4kph in Edinburgh. |
| *Thursday*<br>*July 18* | NASA is selling genuine made-in-space polystyrene! 30,000,000 tiny spheres, produced on board the space shuttle *Challenger* cost £272! |
| *Friday*<br>*July 19* | The *Mary Rose* sank on this day in 1545. Icebergs and thick fog delay the start of *Virgin Atlantic Challenger*'s attempt on the Atlantic speed record in New York. New Moon |
| *Saturday*<br>*July 20* | Ching Ching (12), the Giant Panda, dies at London Zoo. She had suffered from stomach problems for the past few years. |
| *Sunday*<br>*July 21* | More than 12,000 people go to the first-ever Sunday horse race meeting in Britain or Ireland at Leopardstown Park, Dublin. |
| *Monday*<br>*July 22* | The British Virgin Islands (population 12,034) issue new stamps showing the pop star Michael Jackson. |
| *Tuesday*<br>*July 23* | 18.3m trimaran *Apricot* arrives back in Plymouth after 17 days, and wins the 2-man round Britain and Ireland yacht race. |
| *Wednesday*<br>*July 24* | The Watercress Steam Train line in Hampshire is officially re-opened today after the track has been rebuilt. |
| *Thursday*<br>*July 25* | 114 ships set off from Margate at the start of the Cutty Sark Tall Ships Race to Zeebrugge. |
| *Friday*<br>*July 26* | Violent storms sweep the north of England, Scotland and Ireland. Six cattle are struck dead in a field in Co. Down. Floods and landslides round Loch Lomond. |

| | |
|---|---|
| *Saturday*<br>*July 27* | The Great British Bike Race starts at Land's End. It finishes at John O'Groat's on Aug 16. Steve Cram breaks the world mile record at Oslo in 3mins 46.31secs. He knocks 1.03secs off Sebastian Coe's time. |
| *Sunday*<br>*July 28* | The Princess of Wales opens the International Stoke Mandeville Paraplegic Games. |
| *Monday*<br>*July 29* | *Challenger* blasts off from Cape Canaveral again: it's the US's 50th manned space flight and the 19th space shuttle. |
| *Tuesday*<br>*July 30* | The Post Office issues 4 new stamps to celebrate 350 years of the Royal Mail.<br>Full Moon—the second of the month! |
| *Wednesday*<br>*July 31* | Mrs Thatcher drives a mechanical digger to scoop up the first tonne of soil at the start of the Broadgate Development in the City of London. |

# Champions of 1985

| | |
|---|---|
| World Monopoly Champion | Jason Bunn |
| Times Crossword Puzzle Champion | Dr John Sykes |
| Bisto Kids | Jane and Anthony Walker |
| Superbrain of Britain | David Edwards |
| Miss World | Miss Iceland |
| British Trivial Pursuits Champion | Helen Fraser |
| Best in Show at Crufts | Champion Montravia Tommy-Gun (poodle) |
| Supreme Champion at Smithfield | Hae Presto (438kg) |
| Pup Of Year | Louline Heartstrain (wire-haired fox terrier) |
| BBC Today Programme's Woman of Year | Princess Anne |
| BBC Today Programme's Man of Year | Bob Geldof |
| *Time* magazine's Man of Year | Deng Xiaoping |
| Best restored station | Damems, Yorkshire |
| Pub of Year | Royal Oak, Yattendon, Berks |
| Tea Place of Year | Polly's, Marlborough |
| International Birdman Champion | Antonio Madonia |
| World Featherweight Boxing Champion | Barry McGuigan |
| European Heavyweight Boxing Champion | Frank Bruno |
| Chorister of Year | Jonathan Cunliffe |
| World Elver-eating Champion | Mark Ryder |
| Mastermind | Ian Meadows |

# August

| | |
|---|---|
| **Thursday**<br>**August 1** | It's 'C' at the beginning of car number-plates from today! And Rolls Royce makes its 100,000th car. Huge forest fires on the Côte d'Azure in the South of France. |
| **Friday**<br>**August 2** | Col Vladimir Dzhanibekov and Viktor Savinykh go for a 5-hour spacewalk and put new power cells in Salyut-7 |
| **Saturday**<br>**August 3** | The Royal National Eisteddfod 1985 opens in Rhyl. National Town Criers' Championship at Hastings: 4 competitors are women. |
| **Sunday**<br>**August 4** | Queen Elizabeth, the Queen Mother, is 85. Steve Cram (24), from Gateshead, breaks the world 2000m record in Budapest in 4mins 51.39secs. It's his 3rd new record in 19 days! |
| **Monday**<br>**August 5** | Kenichi Horie (46) reaches Japan after sailing alone across the Pacific from Honolulu in a 9m solar-powered boat. It took him 75 days. |
| **Tuesday**<br>**August 6** | One minute's silence in Hiroshima at 8.15am, to mark the 40th anniversary of the dropping of the first atomic bomb. |
| **Wednesday**<br>**August 7** | Nigel Short (20), from Bolton, becomes the first Briton ever to qualify for the world chess championship tournament in Switzerland in October. |
| **Thursday**<br>**August 8** | Westminster City Council put a preservation order on the Victorian Parrot House at London Zoo. |
| **Friday**<br>**August 9** | 500 white doves of peace are released in Nagasaki to mark the 40th anniversary of the dropping of the second atomic bomb on the city. |
| **Saturday**<br>**August 10** | Work stops on a new £47,000,000 container terminal at Felixstowe, Suffolk, after more than 20 rare terns lay eggs there. |
| **Sunday**<br>**August 11** | Edinburgh Festival opens. Heavy rain and Force 8 gales. More than 100 yachts retire from the Fastnet Race. Simon Le Bon, of the pop group Duran Duran, is rescued off Cornwall after his yacht capsizes. |
| **Monday**<br>**August 12** | 19.8m catamaran *Virgin Atlantic Challenger* sets off from New York in a bid to break the Atlantic speed record of 3 days 1hr 40mins, set by the *SS United States* in 1952. |
| **Tuesday**<br>**August 13** | *Virgin Atlantic Challenger* meets some icebergs off Newfoundland. Peter Johnson (28), from Texas, swims the English Channel in 8hrs 20mins—14mins faster than the record set last year. |

| | |
|---|---|
| *Wednesday*<br>*August 14* | Thomas Greene (Maryland, US) eats 1kg snails in 2mins 43.95secs and wins the Champion Snail Eater title. He knocks more than 1min off the record set by Peter Dowdeswell (Northants) last year! |
| *Thursday*<br>*August 15* | *Virgin Atlantic Challenger* is holed and sinks 160km from the Bishop's Rock on the Isles of Scilly. A MAYDAY distress signal is put out at 6.20am and the crew is picked up by a banana boat. |
| *Friday*<br>*August 16* | The Indian government bans the export of human skeletons. Seventh annual Bristol International Balloon Fiesta.<br>New Moon |
| *Saturday*<br>*August 17* | Zola Budd, the South African athlete who was given a British passport last year, breaks the British and Commonwealth 3000m record in 8mins 35.32secs at the European Cup in Moscow, barefoot.<br>22.4°C at Kinlochewe, Highlands |
| *Sunday*<br>*August 18* | Antonio Madonia flies 62m off the end of the pier to win the International Birdman Rally at Bognor, Sussex. |

# *August*

Named in honour of the Roman Emperor Augustus, whose lucky month it was.
The old Dutch name was 'Oost-maand'—harvest month.
The old Saxon name was 'Weodmonath'—weed month.

# Virgin Atlantic Challenger

*Virgin Atlantic Challenger* has two 1200-horsepower engines and burns 4.5 litres of fuel every 25 seconds. There are 14 tonnes of diesel on board but three refuelling stops will be needed in mid-Atlantic. The distance between the Ambrose Light in New York Harbour and the Bishop Rock Light in the Isles of Scilly is 2949 nautical miles.

### *Unlikely Precious Deer*

Père David's deer are named after a Jesuit priest, Père Armand David. In Chinese they are called *Ssupu-Hsiang*, which means 'four unlikes', because they have tails like donkeys, antlers like deer, necks like camels and hooves like oxen! The very first Père David's deer were sent from China to Woburn in 1894.

| | |
|---|---|
| Monday<br>August 19 | The tunnel under the Pennines between Todmorden and Little-borough, which was closed by fire last December, re-opens today. |
| Tuesday<br>August 20 | NASA say that they will build a platform in space, to be called the Industrial Space Facility, in 1989. |
| Wednesday<br>August 21 | Zola Budd breaks the UK mile record in 4mins 17.57secs at Zurich, barefoot. Skegness Council announces the demolition of the 104-year-old pier, 7yrs after it was separated from the shore by a storm! |
| Thursday<br>August 22 | 500th anniversary of the Battle of Bosworth Field. A new statue of Richard III goes on show at Mme Tussaud's in London—without a hunched back or withered arm. |
| Friday<br>August 23 | 22 rare Père David's deer, from Woburn Abbey, Beds, fly to China on an Air France jet. They've been extinct there for nearly 40yrs. |
| Saturday<br>August 24 | St Bartholomew's Day. The Otter Trust at Earsham, Norfolk, announces that otters released into the Broads have bred for the second year running. |
| Sunday<br>August 25 | The £30,000,000 Scottish Exhibition and Conference Centre on the Clyde in Glasgow opens to the public. |
| Monday<br>August 26 | Bank Holiday. No rain in London today—for the first time this month! Zola Budd breaks the world 5000m record at Crystal Palace in 14mins 48.07secs, barefoot. |
| Tuesday<br>August 27 | *Discovery* lifts off from Cape Canaveral at 11.58am BST, in appalling weather conditions, on the 20th US space shuttle mission. |
| Wednesday<br>August 28 | Derrick Amies (41), from Great Yarmouth, catches a 1.2m pike which weighs 18.6kg on the Norfolk Broads—a British record! |
| Thursday<br>August 29 | Amanda Tucker (24), from Aberporth, Dyfed, and Mike McCarthy (25), from Wood Green, London, parachute 91.4m from the top of the Hilton Hotel, London, to try for the shortest parachute drop record! |
| | -0.2°C at Kindrogan, Tayside |
| Friday<br>August 30 | A state of emergency is declared along the coast of the Gulf of Mexico as Hurricane Elena advances at 160kph. |
| Saturday<br>August 31 | Shuttle astronauts William Fisher and James Van Hoften make a 7hr 1min space walk—a US record! They also start repairing a Navy satellite which has been drifting in space since April. |

# September

| | |
|---|---|
| *Sunday*<br>*September 1* | Three communications satellites are launched during US space shuttle *Discovery*'s mission—also one screwdriver, which floats out of the craft and into orbit! |
| *Monday*<br>*September 2* | The National Hurricane Centre in Miami categorises Elena a Major Grade 3 Hurricane. She roars inland at over 200kph. A Franco–American expedition finds the wreck of the *Titanic*, which sank in 1912, off the coast of Newfoundland. |
| *Tuesday*<br>*September 3* | Princess Anne becomes the first member of the Royal Family to take part in a live phone-in—on Radio 4's 'Tuesday Call'. |
| *Wednesday*<br>*September 4* | The *City of Truro*, the world's first 160kph steam engine, goes back into service on the Severn Valley Railway, Shropshire, to celebrate the 150th anniversary of the Great Western Railway. |
| *Thursday*<br>*September 5* | Ken Livingstone, leader of the Greater London Council, parakites 15.2m in the air and lands in the Thames to publicise Thamesday on Saturday. |
| *Friday*<br>*September 6* | A new £44,000,000 reservoir at Grimwith, nr Grassington, is opened. It covers 150 hectares and is the largest in Yorkshire. |
| *Saturday*<br>*September 7* | The last GLC Thamesday. Charlton Athletic Football Club announces that it will leave the ground at the Valley, and join Crystal Palace at Selhurst Park. |
| *Sunday*<br>*September 8* | Dr John Sykes wins *The Times* Crossword Championship for the 8th time! He does 4 puzzles in just under 8½mins each. |
| *Monday*<br>*September 9* | Rabbits are ruining the crops on the Isle of Man so, from today, the Board of Agriculture and Fisheries are paying 35p for each tail. |
| *Tuesday*<br>*September 10* | Monsieur Yvol Le Caer (50) pedals more than 96km across the English Channel from Cherbourg to Poole, Dorset, in just under 17hrs on an aqua-bicycle. |
| *Wednesday*<br>*September 11* | A US scientific satellite, launched 7yrs ago, goes through the tail of the comet Giacobini-Zinner, about 70,796,000km above earth. |
| *Thursday*<br>*September 12* | Wildlife Link report says that otters, great crested newts and smooth snakes are still declining and that there are only 700 pairs of corncrake and 500 pairs of merlin left in Britain. |
| *Friday*<br>*September 13* | A week-long home defence exercise called 'Brave Defender' ends with 200 parachute troops dropping nr Stanford, Norfolk. |

| | |
|---|---|
| *Saturday*<br>*September 14* | The biggest wedding cake in the world is baked in Thailand. It is 13.7m high and has 70 tiers made out of 10,000 eggs, more than 240kg of butter, nearly 200kg of flour and 236 litres of milk!<br><br>27°C in Cambridge     New Moon |
| *Sunday*<br>*September 15* | Europe beats the US and wins the Ryder Cup at the Belfry, Sutton Coldfield for the first time in 28yrs. Steve Ovett wins the Westminster Mile road race in 3mins 56.1secs. |
| *Monday*<br>*September 16* | Switzerland becomes the first country in Europe to make catalytic converters, which need lead-free petrol, compulsory for private cars. |
| *Tuesday*<br>*September 17* | An earth tremor shakes buildings on the Clyde, near the nuclear submarine bases at Faslane and Holy Loch. |
| *Wednesday*<br>*September 18* | A new 10km section of the M25 near Heathrow Airport is opened. Two-thirds of the orbital motorway round London is now complete. Very heavy rain in Scotland: Paisley (Strathclyde) has 74mm. |
| *Thursday*<br>*September 19* | A huge earthquake hits Mexico: the epicentre, 64km off the Pacific coast, measures 8.5 on the Richter Scale.  RICHTER SCALE |
| *Friday*<br>*September 20* | The level of the holy water at the Roman Catholic shrine at Lourdes is very low because of drought. |
| *Saturday*<br>*September 21* | Part of a Wellington bomber called 'R for Robert' is raised from the bottom of Loch Ness. It was ditched in a snow storm on New Year's Eve 1940. |
| *Sunday*<br>*September 22* | The 100-year-old aqueduct on the Grand Union Canal at Weedon, Northants, is closed to boats for 6 weeks for repairs. |
| *Monday*<br>*September 23* | Members of the Magic Circle unveil a plaque to the famous 19th century magician John Nevile Maskelyne in Piccadilly, London, on the site of the old Egyptian Hall.<br><br>More heavy rain in Scotland—it's the worst summer there since 1868 |
| *Tuesday*<br>*September 24* | The Jaguar car is 50 years old. Jason Bunn (25), from Leeds, wins the World Monopoly Championship at Atlantic City, New Jersey. |
| *Wednesday*<br>*September 25* | Archaeologists discover an Iron Age burial chariot at Garton-on-the-Wolds, nr Driffield, Humberside. |
| *Thursday*<br>*September 26* | Two Soviet cosmonauts, Vladimir Dzhanibekov and Georgy Grechko, return to Earth from the orbiting space station Salyut-7. |

| | |
|---|---|
| *Friday*<br>*September 27* | Hurricane Gloria hits New York at nearly 210kph. A BR InterCity diesel sets a new world record by covering the 432km from Newcastle to London in 2hrs 19½mins. |
| *Saturday*<br>*September 28* | The 43,443km Whitbread Round The World Yacht Race starts on the Solent at noon. |
| *Sunday*<br>*September 29* | The Royal Victoria Pier at Ventnor, Isle of Wight, catches fire. There is more than £500,000 damage.<br>Full Moon |
| *Monday*<br>*September 30* | The first British National Guide Dog Week. Dr Charles Richter, who invented the earthquake scale, dies in Pasadena, aged 85. |

# *September*

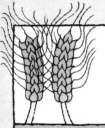

This was the seventh month when the year used to start in March.
The old Dutch name was 'Herst-maand'—autumn month and the old Saxon name was 'Gerst-monath'—barley month.

# National Guide Dog Week

The original guide dogs were almost always Alsatians—or German Shepherds, as they are also called. Now, Labradors, Labrador–Golden Retriever crosses and pure-bred Golden Retrievers are mostly used.

**September 3:** The Post Office issues 4 new Arthurian legends stamps. They mark the 500th anniversary of the printing of Sir Thomas Malory's '*Morte d'Arthur*'.

KING ARTHUR AND MERLIN — 17ᴾ

THE LADY OF THE LAKE — 22ᴾ

GUINEVERE AND LANCELOT — 31ᴾ

SIR GALAHAD — 34ᴾ

# October

| | |
|---|---|
| *Tuesday*<br>*October 1* | Frank Bruno (UK), knocks out Anders Eklund (Sweden), , and wins the European heavyweight championship at Wembley. |
| *Wednesday*<br>*October 2* | Nottingham Goose Fair. Roland Rat deserts TV-AM and joins the BBC. A Cosmos 1686 satellite, launched last Friday, docks with Salyut-7. |
| *Thursday*<br>*October 3* | US space shuttle *Atlantis* blasts off from Cape Canaveral on her maiden voyage—a secret military mission. |
| *Friday*<br>*October 4* | An earthquake in Tokyo measures 6.2 on the Richter Scale. British Telecom put their telephone charges up by an average 3.7%. |
| *Saturday*<br>*October 5* | Friends of the Earth says that acid rain is damaging beech and yew trees. |
| *Sunday*<br>*October 6* | A Punch and Judy Festival in Covent Garden, London, celebrates the 223rd anniversary of the first Punch and Judy show, which was held outside St Paul's Church. |
| *Monday*<br>*October 7* | Traffic is delayed for 5hrs when a 15cm pothole appears in the new section of the M25, opened yesterday! Alderman William Allan Davies will be the next Lord Mayor of London. |
| *Tuesday*<br>*October 8* | The Post Office issues 5 new stamps to celebrate British Film Year.<br>Snow in the Highlands and Cairngorms |
| *Wednesday*<br>*October 9* | Princess Anne drives one of the Army's new 24-tonne MCV80 armoured personnel carriers at Battlesbury Barracks nr Warminster, Wilts. |
| *Thursday*<br>*October 10* | An international garden of peace called 'Strawberry Fields' in Central Park, New York, is dedicated to John Lennon. |
| *Friday*<br>*October 11* | The Queen visits Belize and eats roast rodent—gibnut, which is the meat of the paca, a jungle animal that looks like a large rat or guinea pig. A gust of wind measures over 160kph at Kirkwall, Orkney. |
| *Saturday*<br>*October 12* | Two lifeguards, Andy Muskett (21) and Gary Shopland (22) fly to South America to run the length of the Andes (7,240km). They will run the equivalent of a marathon every day and carry 18kg back packs. |
| *Sunday*<br>*October 13* | Mrs Thatcher is 60. 128 contestants take part in the World Conker Championships at Ashton, near Oundle, Cambs.  |

# October

From the Latin word 'octo' which means eight: it used to be the eighth month in the old Roman calendar.
It was known as 'Winter-fylleth' in Old English, which means winter full moon.

## Happy Birthday Monopoly!

Monopoly celebrates its 50th birthday with a Monopoly Marathon in London on October 20. It starts at the real Marylebone Station at 11am: players have to visit all the places mentioned on the Monopoly Board and get back to Marylebone by 4.45pm, in time to blow out the candles on a huge Monopoly cake! They can use any form of transport they want to.

A lesser-known Monopoly fact is that special sets were made during World War II and sent to prisoners of war. They contained secret maps of escape routes, tiny compasses, fine quality files and real money!

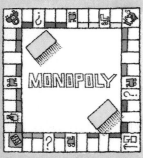

### Broad-leaved Trees

| | |
|---|---|
| Alder | Hornbeam |
| Ash | Oak |
| Beech | Sweet Chestnut |
| Birch | Sycamore |
| Hazel | Willow |

**October 1:** The Forestry Commission offers farmers up to £1 for each traditional broad-leaf tree they plant.

**October 8:** PO issues stamps to honour British Film Year

| | |
|---|---|
| Monday<br>October 14 | A team of divers starts a survey of the wreck of *SS Richard Montgomery*, which sank off Sheerness in 1944. New Moon |
| Tuesday<br>October 15 | The Jubilee Sailing Trust's 400-tonne training ship *Lord Nelson* is launched at Wivenhoe, Essex. The 3-masted barque will be sailed by a mixed crew of physically-handicapped and able-bodied people. |
| Wednesday<br>October 16 | Matthew Rix (10), from Downham Market, Norfolk, names a BR locomotive *Velocity* at Euston Station, London. He won a BBC TV competition! |
| Thursday<br>October 17 | A special party to celebrate the Volkswagen Beetle's 50th birthday is held at Wolfsburg, West Germany. |
| Friday<br>October 18 | An exhibition opens at the Imperial War Museum, London, in memory of Rex, a sniffer dog, who rescued more than 60 people in the Blitz. He was awarded the Dickin Medal (the Animals' VC) in 1945. |
| Saturday<br>October 19 | Motorfair '85 opens at Earls Court, London. 12 teams take part in the annual Cider Barrel Rolling Race at Taunton, Somerset. They have to roll empty 9-gallon barrels over a 2.4km course. |
| Sunday<br>October 20 | Monopoly's 50th birthday is celebrated in London. The Prince and Princess of Wales are interviewed by Sir Alastair Burnett on ITV. About 750,000,000 people watch. |
| Monday<br>October 21 | The King of Tonga (139.8kg) drives to Heathrow airport in a car with the number plate 1 TON and flies to Rotterdam in two seats on a KLM Fokker Fellowship F28 aircraft. |
| Tuesday<br>October 22 | Ten King penguins from Antarctica, which were saved from Taiwanese fishermen, arrive at the Birdland Sanctuary, Bourton-on-the-Water, Gloucs, after 38 days in quarantine. |
| Wednesday<br>October 23 | Bob Geldof, who organised Live Aid, talks to Euro MPs at the European Parliament in Strasbourg about aid for Africa. |
| Thursday<br>October 24 | Women stage a 24-hour strike against male privilege in Iceland. President Finnbogadottir takes part! |
| Friday<br>October 25 | Barry McGuigan, the world featherweight boxing champion, opens two religiously integrated schools for Roman Catholics and Protestants in Belfast—Hazlewood Primary School and Hazlewood College. |

| | |
|---|---|
| *Saturday*<br>*October 26* | In a special ceremony, the Australian government gives Ayers Rock in the Northern Territory back to the Aborigines. It's 335m high and more than 8km round! |
| *Sunday*<br>*October 27* | Holidaymakers are banned from the beach at Ainsdale, nr Southport, Merseyside, to protect the rare species of sand lizard that lives there. British Summer Time ends at 2am: clocks go back 1hr to Greenwich Mean Time. |
| *Monday*<br>*October 28* | A robot drinks butler, built at Campion School, Leamington Spa, wins the Schools Buildarobot Competition at Arborfield, nr Reading.<br><br>Full Moon |
| *Tuesday*<br>*October 29* | An earthquake in Mexico City measures 5.7 on the Richter Scale. There are also tremors in Iran, Algeria and Papua, New Guinea. Lester Piggot (49) rides his last 5 races at Nottingham and retires. He's ridden 4349 winners. |
| *Wednesday*<br>*October 30* | Thames TV's 24-hour Telethon raises £2,500,000 for children's charities. A full-sized replica of Drake's *Golden Hind* runs aground at the mouth of the river Avon. |
| *Thursday*<br>*October 31* | Hallowe'en. Roy Castle tries to tap his foot 1,000,000 times in 24hrs to raise £1,000,000 for charity. All bids for the Channel tunnel (or bridge, or tunnel and bridge) have to be in by midnight. |

## ChatterBox
SIR CLIVE SINCLAIR'S C5 COMPANY GOES BROKE

## Good Egg
POLICEMAN KILLED IN NORTH LONDON RIOT

## TOWN CRIER
MYXOMATOSIS STRIKES PET RABBITS IN SOUTH

## Spotlight
PROTEST AT ACID RAIN: FRIENDS OF THE EARTH COVER TRAFALGAR SQUARE LIONS WITH PLASTIC

# 1985 was . . .

**A Good Year** for Sunday roast chicken, Bob Geldof, Halley's Comet, British films, Nipper, the Heath Fritillary, Jellybeans.

**A Bad Year** for mackerel in Cornwall, the C5, Austrian wine, *Virgin Atlantic Challenger*, plastic pound notes, Coca-Cola's new flavour, rabbits on the Isle of Man.

# November

| | |
|---|---|
| *Friday*<br>*November 1* | A special 136kg cake in the shape of an aircraft carrier is made in Portsmouth to celebrate the commissioning of *HMS Ark Royal*. |
| *Saturday*<br>*November 2* | Robert Swan (28), from Durham, Roger Mear (35)), from Birmingham and Gareth Wood (33), from Edinburgh, set off from their base camp at Cape Evans to retrace Captain Scott's journey to the South Pole. |
| *Sunday*<br>*November 3* | The annual London to Brighton veteran car run starts in Hyde Park. 330 vehicles, all built before 1905, take part. |
| *Monday*<br>*November 4* | Humphrey, a 45-tonne humpback whale, who got stuck over 110km up the Sacramento river while migrating south from Alaska, is lured downstream by a recording of other whales feeding, played underwater from a motor boat! |
| *Tuesday*<br>*November 5* | Humphrey swims out under the Golden Gate Bridge into the Pacific Ocean after 26 days in the Sacramento river. |
| *Wednesday*<br>*November 6* | State Opening of Parliament 11.30am. A street in Hereford is going to be called Geldof Grove, after Bob Geldof, who organised the Live Aid concert. A gust of wind measures 120kph at Fleetwood, Lancs |
| *Thursday*<br>*November 7* | A wax model of Edmond Halley of comet fame goes on show in the Astronomers' Gallery at the London Planetarium. |
| *Friday*<br>*November 8* | Northaird Point, a 21-storey block on the Trowbridge Estate in Hackney, London, is knocked down with a ball and chain. Experts tried to demolish it with 90kg of gelignite on Sunday, but left it looking a bit like the Leaning Tower of Pisa. |
| *Saturday*<br>*November 9* | The Lord Mayor's Show in London. Launch of National Astronomy Week, as Halley's Comet re-appears after 76 years! It should be possible to see it next week, if the skies are clear. |
| *Sunday*<br>*November 10* | Remembrance Sunday. Halley's Comet is now only 120,675,000km from Earth! First snow and ice over most of the country. 1°C at Inverness. Force 10 Gales |
| *Monday*<br>*November 11* | The Prince and Princess of Wales visit Washington, where a special mural of the Princess has been made out of 10,000 jellybeans. |
| *Tuesday*<br>*November 12* | West Yorkshire County Council announces a £10,000,000 scheme to reintroduce trolleybuses in Leeds.  New Moon |

This was the ninth month in the Roman calendar when the year started in March. The Old Saxon name was 'Wind-monath'—wind month—and the Old Dutch name was 'Slaght-maand'—slaughter month.

## Hallo Halley's Comet!

Halley's Comet was first observed by the Chinese in 240BC, and it has been back 32 times since then. The Normans saw it before the Battle of Hastings in 1066 and recorded it in the Bayeux Tapestry. It was observed here in 1628 by the Astronomer Royal, John Flamsteed, and by Edmond Halley, who was the first person to work out that the comet travelled in a huge orbit and not in a straight line. He predicted that it would return in 76 years—and it did!

This year five spacecraft are launched to meet Halley's Comet early in '86: they are the European Space Agency's *Giotto*, Japan's *Suisei* and *Sakigake* and the Soviet Union's *Vega 1* and *Vega 2*. Also launched this year are lots of Halley's Comet souvenirs, complete with official logo. They include plates, glasses, tankards, headscarves, watches and water-clocks. There is a special Halley's Comet Society and an official theme tune—the Halley's Comet Rag!

The comet slowly comes into view over Europe, North America and Asia. It gets brighter during October and November and observers first spot it passing near the Pleiades star cluster. It's not quite as bright as expected, and takes rather a long time to develop a tail!

### Daily Bugle
GARY KASPAROV IS WORLD CHESS CHAMPION

### The Beaver
HALLEY'S COMET FEVER STRIKES, COMPLETE WITH OFFICIAL LOGO AND THEME TUNE

### EAVESDROPPER
THE ROYAL GREENWICH OBSERVATORY STOPS KEEPING BRITAIN'S TIME: IT CAN'T AFFORD TO REPLACE 6 ATOMIC CLOCKS INSTALLED IN 1966

### Daily Scribble
1P CUT IN BASIC 2ND-CLASS POST

**November 3:** Ivan Lendl beats John McEnroe in the European Champions' Championship Final in Antwerp and wins a gold tennis racket encrusted with 1,421 diamonds.

| | |
|---|---|
| *Wednesday*<br>*November 13* | David Frydman, from Wembley, sees Halley's Comet. It's the first British sighting! The world's first wind-powered cruise liner, the *Wind Star*, is launched at Le Havre. |
| *Thursday*<br>*November 14* | The Prince of Wales is 37. There is a massive eruption at the Nevado del Ruiz volcano in Colombia at 2am. |
| *Friday*<br>*November 15* | Beginning of National Tree Week: the Duke of Kent plants a tree in Hyde Park and then goes to a special Tree Council dinner at the House of Lords. |
| *Saturday*<br>*November 16* | The restoration of King Henry VIII's gatehouse at St Bartholomew's Hospital, Smithfield, London, is finished. It's supposedly made out of stone left over from St Paul's Cathedral and contains the only statue of Henry VIII in London. |
| *Sunday*<br>*November 17* | Finals of the Trampolining World Cup at Crystal Palace National Sports Centre, Norwood, start at 2pm. |
| *Monday*<br>*November 18* | The Giftgram is launched at 3500 Post Offices in London and the south east of England. You can send anything—from flying lessons to computer games! |
| *Tuesday*<br>*November 19* | The Post Office issues 5 new Christmas stamps showing Pantomime Characters. |
| *Wednesday*<br>*November 20* | British Rail is going to run special Christmas trains this year from Marylebone Station, London, complete with Santa Claus, balloons and music! |
| *Thursday*<br>*November 21* | Hurricane Kate hits NW Florida and SE Georgia at 160kph. Dr Barnado's Champion Children of the Year lunch at the Savoy. |
| *Friday*<br>*November 22* | The annual Christmas tree for Trafalgar Square, London, arrives from Norway at Felixstowe. It is given a special police guard because 2yrs ago vandals cut off the top. |
| *Saturday*<br>*November 23* | Joan Collins switches on the Christmas lights in Regent's Street, London, at 5pm. |
| *Sunday*<br>*November 24* | Thousands of Muslims gather in Hyde Park to celebrate the birth of the prophet Muhammad, more than 1400 years ago. Their prayers are beamed by satellite all over the world. The Christmas tree goes up in Trafalgar Square. |

| | |
|---|---|
| *Monday*<br>*November 25* | Model skyscrapers go on show at Interbuild at the NEC, Birmingham, to celebrate their centenary. The first skyscraper, the Home Insurance Company Headquarters, was completed 100yrs ago. |
| *Tuesday*<br>*November 26* | A new greenhouse, which recreates 10 different habitats from desert to mangrove swamp, is unveiled at the Royal Botanical Gardens, Kew. |
| *Wednesday*<br>*November 27* | Ford's Granada Scorpio wins the Car of the Year Award. Two 4.8km laser beams point towards Halley's Comet from the roofs of the Mayfair and Kensington Hilton Hotels in London from 6pm–11pm. <br>Full Moon |
| *Thursday*<br>*November 28* | The crew of the US shuttle *Atlantis*, launched on Nov 26, celebrate Thanksgiving with a special dinner of rehydrated chicken consommé, smoked turkey irradiated with gamma rays and thermo-stabilised cranberry sauce. |
| *Friday*<br>*November 29* | Ian Botham reaches Land's End, after walking more than 1,400km from John O'Groats for charity. It took him 35 days. |
| *Saturday*<br>*November 30* | St Andrews Day. 271 Bewick's Swans arrived at the Wildfowl Trust, Slimbridge, Gloucs, this month—the highest number ever in November. Heavy rain in the north of England, Scotland and Northern Ireland. |

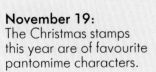

**November 27:**
Hailstones measuring 10–20mm in diameter fall at Lerwick, Shetland. Heavy Snow—20cms in Huntley, Aberdeenshire. Roads are closed in Wales.

**November 19:**
The Christmas stamps this year are of favourite pantomime characters.

# December

**Sunday**
**December 1**

Children's Royal Variety Performance at the Dominion Theatre, London. The costs of removing wheel clamps from cars goes up from £19.50 to £25.

**Monday**
**December 2**

Ian Botham does a 19km lap of honour in London after his marathon walk from John O'Groats to Land's End in aid of the Leukaemia Research Fund.

**Tuesday**
**December 3**

The US space shuttle *Atlantis* lands safely in California after its 7-day mission.

**Wednesday**
**December 4**

The Queen and 5 former prime ministers go to dinner with Mrs Thatcher at No 10 Downing Street to celebrate its 250th birthday as the Prime Minister's official residence. It was given to Sir Robert Walpole by King George II.

**Thursday**
**December 5**

A 198-year-old bottle of wine, a 1787 Chateau Lafitte, is sold at Christie's in London for £105,000. It was originally owned by Thomas Jefferson, 3rd President of the USA.

**Friday**
**December 6**

Edward Leigh (Con) MP for Gainsborough and Horncastle, loses a tooth while making a speech about violent crime among the young.

**Saturday**
**December 7**

A black and white warbler from Venezuela is spotted in Potter Heigham, Norfolk.

**Sunday**
**December 8**

Alan Saldhana (8) wins the Save the Children Fund Scrabble Championship for under 10s in London—for the 2nd year running.

**Monday**
**December 9**

Britain's heaviest turkey (35kg), is sold for £3500 at the Butchers' Hall, London. If the skies are clear, you should be able to see Halley's Comet this week. It's about 96,540,000km from earth now.

**Tuesday**
**December 10**

A French report to the European Parliament in Strasbourg suggests that British chocolate should be renamed 'vegelate' or 'industrial chocolate' because it contains 5% vegetable fats.

**Wednesday**
**December 11**

250,000 people are without water in Leeds because of a burst water main. Schools close and soldiers provide emergency supplies.

**Thursday**
**December 12**

A new Brown Dog Memorial is unveiled in Battersea Park, London. The original bronze statue, which was presented to the Borough by the International Anti-Vivisection Council, was removed and melted down after huge riots in 1907.

New Moon

| | |
|---|---|
| *Friday*<br>*December 13* | Six NATO minesweepers and minehunters go through the Thames Barrier and the Pool of London, to berth alongside *HMS Belfast*. |
| *Saturday*<br>*December 14* | Mrs Anne Mallinson, deputy chairman of the City of London Magistrates, is going to be the next Lord Mayor of Westminster. She will be the second woman to hold this office. |
| *Sunday*<br>*December 15* | Barry McGuigan, the world featherweight boxing champion, is named BBC TV's Sports Personality of the Year. Cloudy skies are going to make it difficult to spot Halley's Comet this week. |
| *Monday*<br>*December 16* | 112,700,000 items are posted today—an all-time record for one day. The Post Office has to take on an extra 32,000 people and 4,000 vehicles. 20th anniversary of the launch of the Pioneer 6 space probe, which is still sending back data as it orbits the sun.  |
| *Tuesday*<br>*December 17* | A new Government-sponsored survey of coastal waters is going to monitor more than 350 seaside resorts for pollution. |
| *Wednesday*<br>*December 18* | The French Government and Walt Disney agree on Europe's first Disneyland park—near Marne-la-Vallée, 25km east of Paris. |

# *December*

X  X

This used to be the tenth month in the Roman calendar when the year started in March.

## The new Brown Dog Statue

The original Brown Dog Statue was put up in Battersea Park, London, in 1906 in memory of a little brown dog who died in the laboratories of University College. It sparked off huge street riots between medical students and anti-vivisectionists. Hundreds of students marched on the statue and tried to destroy it but large crowds of animal lovers defended it. A 24-hour police guard had to be mounted but, in 1907, the bronze statue was torn down, taken away and melted down. The new statue is made by Nicola Hicks and is modelled on her own Jack Russell terrier.

| | |
|---|---|
| *Thursday*<br>*December 19* | Last posting day for first-class Christmas cards! US space shuttle *Columbia*'s launch is postponed 14secs before lift-off when a fault is detected in the booster rocket steering system. |
| *Friday*<br>*December 20* | Topping-Out ceremony at the Swan Theatre, Stratford-upon-Avon. |
| *Saturday*<br>*December 21* | Winter solstice 10.08pm. The sun rises at 8.06am and sets at 3.51pm which makes it the shortest day of the year—only 7hrs 45mins! |
| *Sunday*<br>*December 22* | A 6m whale is found washed up on the beach at Pett Level, nr Hastings. The river Ouse bursts its banks in York after the water level rises by more than 3.5m. |
| *Monday*<br>*December 23* | The glare of the moon makes it difficult to see Halley's Comet, which is in the constellation of Aquarius. |
| *Tuesday*<br>*December 24* | Christmas trees cost about £1.50 for each 30.5cms in shops this year. Most of them are Norway Spruce, although Scots pine, the noble fir and the caucasian fir are becoming more popular. |
| *Wednesday*<br>*December 25* | Christmas Day. The Queen's Christmas message is beamed by satellite to Europe for the first time. 132 people take part in the charity Christmas swim at Hunstanton, Norfolk, and raise £1500. |
| *Thursday*<br>*December 26* | The Thames Flood Barrier is raised for only the second time ever at 9.43pm, because of very high tides driven by gale force winds. |
| *Friday*<br>*December 27* | The Thames Barrier is lowered at 2am, as the winds subside. A tricycle made for 21 leaves Buckingham Palace at the start of a sponsored ride from London to Paris. Full Moon |
| *Saturday*<br>*December 28* | China's leader Deng Xiaoping is named *Time* magazine's 1985 Man of the Year.<br><br>One of the coldest weekends this year, with temperatures down to -14°C. Snow in Wales, Scotland, NE England and East Anglia. |
| *Sunday*<br>*December 29* | *The Flying Scotsman* steams out of Marylebone Station, London, on its way to Stratford-upon-Avon. |
| *Monday*<br>*December 30* | David, a Brazilian tapir, and Azraq, a rare Arabian oryx, who were both born at London Zoo over Christmas, make their first public appearance. |
| *Tuesday*<br>*December 31* | Princess Anne and Bob Geldof are voted Personalities of the Year by BBC Radio 4's 'Today' programme. |